LONDON IN VERSE

PATRICK CLARE

JANUS PUBLISHING COMPANY
London, England

First published in Great Britain 1997
by Janus Publishing Company,
Edinburgh House, 19 Nassau Street,
London W1N 7RE
Copyright © Patrick Clare 1997

British Library Cataloguing-in-Publication Data.
A catalogue record for this book is available from the
British Library.

ISBN 1 85756 371 9

Cover design Harold King

Printed & bound in England by Antony Rowe

Phototypeset by Intype London Ltd.

The Metropolis

To the great metropolis they come
from all corners of the globe
to the great metropolis they come
in various forms of robe
from the far off hills of India
or from the plains of Pakistan
from the tropics of Africa
they will come if they can

To the Irish navvy, not now cutting peat
but digging up a London street
To the man from the valleys
speaking with a soft lilt
or the man from the Highlands
with his bagpipes and his kilt
perhaps, remembering that tale of old
to come and look for London's gold

To the Chinese who run a restaurant
to the American who comes to flaunt
to the wine drinking Frenchman
and the sausage eating German
to the Italian making spaghetti
and the Greek and Turk in their community
the man from Jamaica, he is there too –
so is the Arab, and so is the Jew

To whatever part of London you may go
Whether to the East End or to Soho
you will be in colourful company

you will meet every nationality
they come from far and wide
as though it were a human tide
in every street and on every thoroughfare
you will find the whole world there

Monstrostopia

'Tis such a pity, that the rebuilding
of this vast and wond'rous City
is turning out to be such a monstrosity
for instead of buildings that are
graceful and fair
we now have horrible things that
are both ugly and square

Ah, if only Wren were alive to see
Oh how unhappy he would be
such monsters, rising so high
as if trying to reach the sky
nothing but slabs of concrete
and sheets of steel
has there ever been anything
with so little appeal?

In front of these buildings stand
insults to sculpture by the modern hand
these fantasies so crude
as if trying, the public to delude
one stands there guessing
at these things so depressing
wishing that one could knock them apart
for, you would hardly call them objects of art

This modern rubble cannot last
like the glorious architecture of the past
for, what can compare, with
St Paul's and Westminster Abbey

surely none of these prefabs so shabby
these projects by the business tycoons
reaching upwards like toy balloons
Oh what a mess! All in the name of progress

City Gent

Ding dong, ding dong,
Big Ben sings his song
to the crowds as they throng, and
to the traffic as it bustles along

Ding dong, ding dong,
'tis a majestic song
for it can be heard above the sound
of the hurry and scurry all around

What a magnificent sight to see
tall and stately is he
and as the people go on their way
he sings out to them the time of day

Many a change there has been
but that stalwart figure can still be seen
and as the years pass along
he continues to sing his lordly song

The London Cabby

To find their way around
this great City
would put most people in a daze
but not so the London cabby
as he zips through London's maze

If there's any place you may
wish to see
anywhere you may want to go
just consult the dear old cabby
for he is bound to know

Maybe to the West End somewhere
to sedate Berkeley Square
or to noisy, Battersea funfair
he's sure to get you there

Perhaps some quaint old pub
or some exclusive night club
some place that's not on the map
just leave it to this worthy chap

Perhaps you have a train to catch
or maybe going to a football match
and the time just seems to sail
he will get you there, without fail

The London cabby is always on the go
come hail, rain or snow
through London's frustrating traffic flow
like beetles scurrying to and fro

Meeting Place

Nelson, on his perch so high
Much can he see, though he has but one eye
the crowds milling in the square below
gathering for a meeting, to tell their
tale of woe

The marchers, they have come to their
journey's end
their liberty to defend
with banners unfurled
proclaiming their grievances to the world

Merry trippers, out for the day
or visitors from far away
come with bread, or maybe seed
come to appease the hungry pigeons' greed

This place of London's pride
a fine thoroughfare as all can see
where people sing at Christmastide
their carols, around Norway's gift
of a giant fir tree

On whatever occasion it may be
whether grave, sorrowful, or happy
it is here, where the revellers meet
it is here the birth of a New Year they greet

Like the mist gathering on the mountains
though the weather be foul or it be fair

they still meet by the fountains here in
Trafalgar Square

The Lane

Come and buy, come and buy
'tis the old familiar cry
and it can be heard time and time again
in London's Petticoat Lane

Here amongst the laden stalls
can be heard various street calls
it is here that you can buy
almost anything under the sky

Anything from a needle,
though, perhaps not a haystack
something for baby's cradle
or a brush to scratch your back

Anything odd or something queer
you will surely find it here
maybe a clock with two faces
or just a pair of shoe laces

Silks and cottons from India
all sorts of toys and humming tops
who knows, a magic carpet from Persia
to whisk you above the roof tops

Cup, saucers, and teapots
all kinds of delft, there are lots
knives, forks and spoons from Hong Kong
and if you want, a Chinese dinner gong

Strange characters you will meet
here in London's Middlesex Street
eating fire as though it were a treat
or treading on glass in bare feet

Here, the eager crowds throng
hoping for something for a song
the traders, with cries the crowd they greet
of bargains, they cannot hope to repeat

To mind your wares you would do well
for, there is a story they do tell
whatever you may lose down the lane
they'll sell it to you as you come out again

The Cockney Sparrow

The cockney sparrow
a perky little chap is he
perched on a coster's barrow
and chirping merrily

In almost any place
can this cheeky fellow be found
in any street or market place
this flighty fellow does abound

Flitting from rooftop to rooftop
as free as he can be
seemingly that he cannot stop
so busy and nosy is he

Hopping and skipping
he never keeps still
hoping for a tasty something
on your window sill

On your doorstep your milk he spies
to him it is free
and that should be no surprise
for, more brazen than his country cousin is he

The Eighth Wonder

Beneath this throbbing city, tracks
and tunnels abound
and no greater engineering feat
can be found, than that of
the London underground
electric locomotives, surging to and fro
like giant centipedes, deep down
in the earth below

Clickety clack, clickety clack
they speed along the hidden track
brightly lit, as they zoom
and pierce the murky gloom
far below the busy street
beneath the millions
of tramping feet

Like the workings of the busy ant
of praise, one cannot recant
for, if in haste to get to town
there is no quicker way
no traffic jam to cause a frown
as you spark along the electric way

These busy motors hum and swing along
like the rhythm of pulsating song
taking thousands to their daily chores
often packed tight, to the doors
rocking on their speedy way
while the crowded straphangers sway

Of the wonders under Heaven
it is said, that there are seven
but, I have heard this said before
that, possibly there is one more
and somehow I am inclined to think
that this may be the missing link

Revered Terrain

Like little Jack Horner
they gather in a corner
at the edge of London's Hyde Park
arguing and debating, until it is quite dark
some come, to tell of the truth
while other come to gibe
and some are quite uncouth
as though from some forgotten tribe

Some come for publicity
while some come to pray
and others talk of liberty
though they know not what they say
some claim to be Heaven sent
others seem to be power bent
and if only given consent
they would get rid of the government

On a platform, above the crowd they tower
how they'd perform, if only
given the power
yes, if they had their way
we'd have utopia without delay
less work and more play
we'd always be happy and
we'd always be gay

By voicing their fiery thoughts aloud
see how they draw the crowd
how they rant, how they rage

how they would turn history's page
whatever they may wish to portray
and some may speak in vain
they are quite free to have their say
here on this revered terrain

Barrow Boy

Oh barrow boy
what is that you cry
a pound of pears I'll buy
your rosy apples I'll try

Ripe tomatoes
Canary beauty
ripe tomatoes
they're fresh and fruity

Ah, barrow boy
those grapes look sweet
a pound you can supply
to give myself a treat

Juicy melons
all fresh and nice
juicy melons
just look at the price

Hardy barrow boy
in the wind and rain
cheerful barrow boy
calling out again

Lovely oranges
from sunny Spain
lovely oranges
buy, while they remain

Busy barrow boy
with sandwiches and flask
to serve the passer-by
for that is his task

Sweet tangerines
do try a few
sweet tangerines
they're so good for you

Oh barrow boy
with your shop on wheels
on barrow boy
I love to hear, your melodic appeals

Portobello Fair

If looking for something unique
some colourful piece of delft
some enchanting and rare antique
to decorate your mantel shelf
come along to this place, behind
Notting Hill Gate
for you are sure to find
something that will fascinate

A dazzling chandelier
to decorate your ceiling
a silver tankard for your beer
when you have that thirsty feeling
and Alpine cattle bell, that may
be all the rage
and one can never tell, something
from the prehistoric age

Some interesting little knick-knack
here amongst the bric-à-brac
a beautiful Japanese fan
jewellery once belonging to a Sultan
or some exotic necklace
your lady's neck to grace
or to make your collection increase
an Indian pipe of peace

Looking for a chair to rock
a gaunt old Grandfather's clock
ornate swords or cutlasses

from the wreck of some pirate ship
some delicate wine glasses
to have a tasty sip
an ancient tribal face mask
or an old Spanish sherry cask

There are so many things here
too numerous to relate
anything from an African spear
to fine old silver plate
a sheepskin hearth rug
to make your fireside snug
at this road with the name so mellow
this road called Portobello

The Oasis

This fair oasis, amidst
the concrete wilderness,
one of London's green places
that colours the City's greyness
to bring a touch of countryside
with these fields so lush
and so to provide
a refuge, to escape the City's crush

Various are the pleasures to be found
here, in the City's playground
a-rowing you may like to go
or trot your horse down Rotten Row
listen to a brass band play
on a lazy Bank Holiday
or hopefully cast your line
from the banks of the Serpentine

How one's heart does gladden
to see the crocus display
here in London's garden
as winter is passing away
or the dainty little snowdrops
a joyful sight to see
as though sheltering from the haildrops
under some gaunt and towering tree

Though one may weary
at the hurry and scurry of the day
but how one's heart is cheery

to see the children romp and play
in this open space, where come picnickers gay
this restful place, to yawn away
the heat of the summer's day

London Waterway

The Thames, rising in Gloucestershire
though it may
but surely this is London's Waterway
weaving and winding through fields of
new-mown hay
and calling at the fair towns of Henley and
Windsor on its zig-zaggy way
a-weaving and winding does it go
'till it reaches the great Metropolis overflow

Flowing gently past Hampton Palace
and its baffling maze
where visitors amble around as if in a daze
and so on to that town once renowned
where the Kings of old were
ceremoniously crowned
and, on a little further still
Oh what a view from Richmond Hill

Leaving behind, the barges heavily laden
at where the little Brent flows in
and while on the Surrey side
those gardens of botanical pride
and from both sides of the banks
a little way upstream from here
the victorious sculling crew receive a
resounding cheer

The bustling borough of Hammersmith
it flanks

with its taverns by its banks
its swing bridge and flyover
the motorist's idea of being in clover
and so to where the footballers engage
on the riverside pitch at Craven Cottage

Gliding along, where once were
meadows and grass
now, one huge sprawling mass
you will see him at Chelsea
where the dreamers stay
and at Battersea with its gardens gay
but surely, this is beyond a joke
its power house belching filthy smoke

Helicopters, like some strange bird
rise into the sky
happy pleasure boats cruising by
the crowded water bus
all adding, to the fuss
but London's river slips by with no
trouble at all, under the busy
bridge at Vauxhall

Still on his journey bent
past the Houses of Parliament
with its much debating members
and Prime Minister
here, at historic and fair Westminster
while, that towering timepiece booms
him a how-do-you-do
as he makes his way to Waterloo

Sweet music, from the festival hall
is played
swirling by where once the Blackfriars
knelt and prayed

under the Capital's bridge, with its
traffic City bound
Never a more exciting river
I'll be bound
past that Tower of dread, where many
an innocent victim lost their head

Harbour and rivercraft toot
the Tower Bridge rising, as if
some ship to salute
and in the dockland, shipping
from every nation, their colourful
emblems displayed
while those loftly cranes on parade
lining the busy wharves
nodding and dipping like giant giraffes

Past London's Oriental quarter
one of its busiest stretches of water
on to Poplar and Greenwich to make
a call
and over the tunnel of Blackwall
following its route like that of
the bygone tram
to fill the tidal basins
of East and West Ham

Looking, from an aeriel view,
like a huge serpent
continuing his journey through
the counties of Essex and Kent
and while the great Metropolis sleeps
it's, as it were, some vigil he keeps
surging along full of energy
on to embrace the mighty sea

London Pride

What a fair and dainty flower
is London pride
its beauty, try as it may,
it cannot hide
Oh what a wonderful and vivid shade
of pink
it makes one stop and wonder
it makes one stop to think

Oh what happiness to the City
dweller does it bring
as it displays its blossoms
in the spring
whether in a garden or on a
window-sill, one's heart it does elate
even a derelict building or ugly
bomb site, does it decorate

Have you ever seen such exquisite
and delicate sprays
adding its colour to the lengthening
days
its flowery beads of pollen
to make sweet and delicious honey
much to the joy and delight
of the busy, City bee

Meat Store

Oh! for the roast beef of
old England
to make your dinner grand
and there are juicy joints galore
here, in London's meat store
and plenty of mutton too
to make a tasty Irish stew
plenty here for the butchers to buy
to fill many a steak and kidney pie

Such succulent meat at hand
coming from many a far-off land
tons upon tons from Argentina
rabbits too from Australia
tender lamb from New Zealand
and all that is best from Scotland
so there's quite an international
flavour
to suit everybody's savour

Hustling porters calling, their
frozen loads, on hand barrows
hauling
with backs bent low
and always on the go
these good men, on whom we rely
to replenish the City's meat supply
for at dawn
while London continues to snore
work begins at this great meat store

Light Blue and Dark Blue

There are few, who could withstand
the gruelling pace
like that of the London boat race
what energy and stamina
it must take
battling from Putney to Mortlake

On a cold and windy March day
the men of Oxford and Cambridge
test their strength and skill
in a sculling fray
these students who make up the crew
each, rowing for a different shade of blue

Oh! what excitement when they appear
with an assorted procession
bringing up the rear
just yards away from the perspiring few
Ah, but what colour is in the lead,
is it the dark, or is it the light hue

How swiftly over the water they glide
these fragile skiffs, built by men
with skill and pride
made, to put both man and craft
to the test
in this tough and exerting contest

Like ghost ships they come silently by
except, for that of their coaches'

clear cut cry
one, as though encouraging their team
to keep their pride of place
the other, urging theirs to a better pace

But what precision as they row
more like clockwork as they go
with the winner, maybe a length to spare
streaking to the post as if in top gear
and so, the battle of the blues
is over, for yet another year

The 'Dilly

Jaunting jolly Piccadilly
where happy visitors meet
colourful gay and frilly
distinct and discreet
where once dwelt the gentry
and once the haunt of dandies
now come all and sundry
licking ice lollies
and chewing sugar candies
swarming along this unique parade
lined with eating places
agencies and bars
or crowding the quaint little shops
in Burlington Arcade
while from the underpass
stream a thousand motor cars
and so to the humming circus
with its centre piece
The Greek God of love
and the buildings roundabout
ablaze with brilliant neons above
here the sporting crowds
congregate happily
some may sing, some may clown
as they all make for the 'dilly
the heart of London town

The Pearlies

Where else will you meet
such personalities?
Like that of the gay pearlies
where else? But this great City
of diversity and variety
what more colourful characters
have you seen
than that of the Pearlie King
and his gracious Queen

The King in his multi-buttoned suit
maybe a street trader selling fruit
his Queen, brightly buttoned too
she also a costermonger true
Oh! what a jolly pair in their
ornate costumes
She also sporting the finest ostrich plumes

In many a London district
you have this royalty elect
and when there's a get together
they don't give a fig
about the weather
indulging in their delightful
cockney crosstalk
or doing the gay and
sprightly Lambeth walk

At any of these gay parties
whatever these kindly folk

may collect, goes to various charities
and if their many buttons
you may try to guess
I'm afraid you won't have much success
for those who wear them do not
forget, and will not tell, for,
it is a closely kept secret

The Old Lady

The Old Lady of Threadneedle Street
a fine old lady is she
always reserved and always discreet
and richer than many can ever be

a London 'native', she has not strayed
still haunting the olden City
her important role still being played
with her millions in the kitty

Though she may be ageing and grey
and having, like all, her faults
she continues strongly to hold sway
with gold and silver in her vaults

If one had thoughts of stealing her wealth
a clever one he'd need to be
he'd have to use cunning and stealth
for, protected by stalwart guardsmen is she

City Church

This City Church, upon the hill
at Ludgate, within the Roman
boundary
gives to visitors a thrill
and a loving memory

Solidly built on high, in
magnificent style, placed
so all could see,
and stop for a while, and
admire its Palladian beauty

Around and about its majestic
dome, cooing pigeons find
their home
and clear above the traffic swell
can be heard its hourly bell

This masterpiece of Sir Christopher
Wren, one of the finer of
craftsmen
and look wherever you may, you
will not find, the like of it today

Flowery Way

If I were to forget Kensington Gardens
I would beg a thousand pardons
for, where else in town on a summer's day
will you find such a brilliant floral array

Flowers here to suit everybody's likes
tall elegant delphinium spikes
broad leafed geraniums
and a many coloured assortment
of antirrhinums

Oh to see too the lupin beauties
and the velvety petals of the pansies
and here too, their beauty unfolds
the orange and lemons of the
African marigolds

A visit here is very well spent
to inhale the stock the sweetest scent
here also the favourite rose
and the fuchsias in their drooping pose

Blossoms here of every colour and shade
such splendour only The Creator has made
blossoms here for everyone to love
like the dainty bells of the
lovely foxglove

Here you will not sadden, but feel gay
as you walk along this flowery way

or relax here, on a garden seat
you will find none better, you will
find no repeat

The Totters

Clip clop, clip clop
away go the totters
clip, clop, clip clop
Oh! the music of their trotters
around at a leisurely trot
from street to street they jog
around at a leisurely trot
while little children stand agog

All kinds of junk
piled upon their carts
all kinds of junk
from tattered rags to motor parts
almost anything they request
as they trundle by
almost anything they request
each with their own enchanting cry

'Tis a long day
both for man and his nag
'tis a long day
with many a laden bag
but he's sure to stop for a pint
and sort out some old coats
but he's sure to stop for a pint
and to give old faithful his oats

On the trot again
after a sugary treat
on the trot again

their breadwinning task to repeat
off home at a steady canter
with a veritable treasure trove

Cup Final

Up for cup, ay, that's what the
Northerners say
as they come, on Cup Final Day
to see their home team play
jostling along with a merry song
down the Empire Way
this carefree and happy throng
surging along with rattles
and rosettes gay

To the Capital they swarm
coming, as if to take it by storm
this sporting arena to fill
like a fairy castle upon a hill
in specially laid on trains
ringing with boisterous refrains
to see a game of football
at the edge of London's great sprawl

Get your colours here, get your programmes
there!
There are people calling everywhere
Oh! the hurly burly
at Suburban Wembley
ice-cream salesmen with their brands
hot dog vendors at their stands
and joining in the hullabaloo newsmen,
with their Special Editions too

A capacity crowd, packed like sardines in

a tin
waiting for the contest to begin
with a martial band to coax them along
the massive choir drifts into song
and as the opposing teams file out
hear them roar, hear them shout!
And too with excitement they bristle
at the shrill note of the referee's whistle

At half time, whichever side may
hold sway, there is still yet time
for the other to win the day
and as they take their rest
military bands parade
and play with zest
and whatever the result at the end of
play,
it is to this sporting crowd,
their one and only day

The rejoicing victors, their awards
being made, in a lap of honour
around the stadium parade
their valiant captain, shoulder high
is he, holding aloft the coveted trophy
and the melting crowds, winners or losers
will not be off to an early bed
but, to the West End to paint the town red

Pageantry

Happy children, edging the City's kerbside
their parents, they're excited too, you know,
have come, a slowly bus or speedy tube ride,
to welcome the new Lord Mayor
and his glittering show

What other pageant excels
what other to compare
as this colourful procession
gets under way with the melodic peal of
Bow Bells
and a blaring trumpet fanfare

Led by a smart and strident band
harmonizing a stirring martial air
to set one's feet a-dancing
and close at their heels
cavalry grand
their trusty steeds a-prancing

All kinds of uniform fill this unique parade
men in naval and flying gear
all branches of the armed profession
whatever grade
even in the garments of yesteryear

What meticulous care it must have
taken to prepare
numerous tableaux, interlaced with various
bands

depicting national prosperity or welfare
a rare treat too, for visitors from other lands

The City dignitaries also play their part
officers of the City Corporation
Mr Sheriff in his carriage
bright and smart
Alderman and Sheriff also
in similar transportation

So too is seen, marching erect, the City
Recorder
preceding the band of the Honourable
Company of Artillery
and his retiring Lordship in following order
to the rear of the musical soldiery

Yet more horsemen go trotting past
also in the saddle, the City Marshal
and in like manner, state trumpeters
heralding the approach,
with musical blast, the newly elected
Mayor in his ornate coach

Hauled along, amidst the excitement and
cheers
by six brewery shires, sturdy and strong
with chaplain, sword-bearer and serjeant-at-arms
in attendance,
escorted all, by pikemen and musketeers

As it rumbles past, antique and golden
Oh! to see the enchanted children's faces
aglow
this final scene, as though from some fairy
tale olden
Oh! the pageantry of the Lord Mayor's Show!

Master Detective

In busy bustling Baker Street
there once lived a sleuth elite
at headquarters 221B, he would greet
his friend and colleague discreet

With some air of professional pride
in Dr. Watson he would confide
always busy, and never slow
with the lawbreaker to lay low

This master detective, whose work
seldom was, if ever defective
it was not like him to fail
when hot on some criminal's trail

Such was his fame, the underworld
would quake at the mention of his name
such was his skill and ability
the idol and toast of society

To the GPO's efficient team, letters
from the world over continue to stream
seeking his aid, to track down some crook
but alas, alack, he was just a character in
a book

'Appy 'Ampstead

'appy 'ampstead as the cockneys say
'appy 'ampstead on a bank holiday
Oh! to picnic on its heath, this lovely
green display
to hear the melodious sound
of its funfair merry and gay,
with its swings, roundabouts and go-carts,
to delight children's little hearts
to spend an hour or two,
to wander through its woodlands and shrubberies
to amble along and hear the many birds sing
twittering and chirping, as though in the
countryside wide,
yet, not far away, the roar and flow of the
traffic tide,
as it hustles through the village with all the
clatter of modern hub-bub
here, this unique garden suburb

News Village, Canary Press (Canary Wharf)

Once situated where the river Fleet
sped by.
This place of news, views and headlines
to catch the public eye.
News from the world wide
continuous rapid and fleet on the
teleprinters ride
though not always too discreet
Exploits in outer space
some by-election pending
for the news hungry populace
their appetite never ending.
Here the national dailies supplying the need
each their headlines hinting
and there are many here indeed
in this place of printing
of caxtons art and skill
this place of news
never seems to be still
place of controversial views
going from here in print
and while the street lamps burn bright
craftsmen tail at their stint
and the presses roar through the night

Blitz

From this aerial onslaught
London did not quail
which destructive machines had wrought
with their load of deadly hail
for in the flarelight glow
this City they sought to raze
this citadel to lay low
with bomb and fiery blaze

To the siren's fearsome wail
searchlights raked the sky
thundering guns at these raiders
on the war trail, let their missiles fly
with crashes resounding through the night
and seeming as if some awesome dream
these marauders to put to flight
caught, silver-like in a crossbeam

In that terrible, yet beautiful
summer of nineteen-forty
when the gallant few, resourceful
took to the air in a daring sortie
dogfighting beneath summery skies
or 'neath the stars shining bright
as though with cat eyes
as they swooped in the night

Many a weary month long
could be heard, the bombs' eerie whistle
but London's heart still beat strong

spurning this odious dismissal
its streets shaking with explosions loud
and shrapnel on its rooftops to rain
but London could still be proud
an indomitable fortress to remain

Fish Market

Busy, fishy Billingsgate
I can smell you a mile away
though not always an odour to irritate
if you ever pass this way
breezy, noisy, but not now by the Thames-side
with laden lorries from many a port
keeping the jolly fishmongers supplied
their diesel engines snort
porters on the go
with boxes of cod, plaice, or bloaters
or other kinds to show
atop their leathery boaters
all kinds, whatever you may wish
for a gourmet to delight
to make a tasty dish
or the shop, that's "frying to-night"!

Botanical London

Some pence, just a few, is all
that one needs, to visit the world
famed gardens at Kew
and how they all come, through
its wrought iron gates
from distant lands and various climates
visitors from the Orient, maybe sheikhs
and other people of leisure
or maybe some from the millions of the
metropolis to admire its charm and
beauty, and make a day of pleasure

You may visit for whatever reason
to seek out some strange plant
or the blossoms of the season
it may be a day of wintry gloom
but you will surely delight
at the shades of heather bloom
and if on a visit in the early
months of the year, do not forget
to look for the delightful beauty
of the dainty snowdrop carpet

How nice, along its pathways to wander
and perhaps stop awhile, joyfully,
to ponder
while sparrows in chirpy batches
flit in and out of the crocus patches
to see the many trees breaking bud,
the joy that it brings, goes without saying

and giving one a further thrill
the narcissi and daffodils
in the March winds nodding and swaying

Here also, lovers bring their sweethearts
to kiss and cuddle amidst
the wonderful joys of spring
beneath trees, their blossom-laden
boughs, looking like candy floss,
in a gentle breeze, as if to them,
their dainty blooms to toss
while round about, the early bees
sip their nourishment, seemingly from the
beautiful lips of the graceful tulips

Summer too, brings its glory
with roses of pink, red, white or tea
of such splendour, one could write
many a story
Oh! to stroll amongst such sweetness
their delightful odour, the long
evening's scenting, as if,
some heavenly brew fermenting
and more of summer's colour
is found here, to excite the nature lover's heart
such goodness, only the good God can impart

You may come here, as the leaves are
tumbling and twirling
and too, when the autumn mists
come swirling
but, when the sun lifts that wispy
veil, the beauty of the varied
foliage unfolds, in their shades
of red, yellow and golds, or you may
leave your footprints in the snow, here,
looking like the cards at Christmas on show

Exotic orchids, plants from all corners
of the earth
of the many kinds, here, there
is no dearth
shrubs and bushes with names so strange
Oh! there is such an extensive range
cactus from the deserts of Mexico
pine, cedar and palm trees, and sticks of
bamboo, from the tropics growing
making such an interesting showing

Oranges, lemons and lime, fruits
which do not grow in this cold
unsettled clime
grow here, in their accustomed warmth
in the vast hothouses, although
the weather outside may be freezing
and the potted plants with all the
colours of the rainbow, making it all
so very pleasing and nice to reside
here, at London's Surrey side

The Wearin' of the Green

Oh! the wearin' of the green, in this
vast City
home now, and 'tis more the pity
of many an exile
from the fair Emerald Isle
'tis heart-warming to be seen
this wearing of the green
with the many shades displayed
in a fine St. Patrick's Parade

Though a Sunday, busy still are
London's streets
as taxis and buses swarm by
in noisy fleets
to be halted for a while
by this procession of green to beguile
with many a kilted and
sparkling band
leading off by London's famous Strand

So through London's fine thoroughfares
are heard many of Erin's national airs
and causing strangers to stop and wonder
the skirl of pipes and drums' thunder
honouring their patron saint
and heroes of yesterday
their journey ending at the fine Cathedral
at Westminster
to kneel to Almighty God and pray

51

So they come, men, women, lads and lassies
from Erin's fertile soil
seeking their fortunes in various
forms of toil
and there's a get-together to chase
their cares away, on the feast of
St. Patrick with many a céli gay
Oh! the wearin' of the green
another part of London's colourful scene

The Little Garden

This little garden, almost hidden
and tucked away
behind Oxford Street's façade gay
where one can escape for awhile
from the never ending traffic file
this peaceful retreat
with pigeons cooing, and sparrows
and starlings which chirp and tweet
as they flock on the grass
awaiting the breadcrumbs
from the people who pass
or those who, as they please
take their ease
on the seats around the flower beds
beneath the trees
which give a pleasant shade
and welcome release
from the humidity
of the crowded atmosphere
so, what place, in the West End here,
is there to match
this little green patch
called Soho Square

The Warriors' Residence

There is, at Chelsea by the Thames-side
a home where elderly warriors reside
they, having put their courage
to the test
their battles over, now in retirement
enjoy a well earned peace and rest
to relax and recall some happening
of an earlier day
whether on the barrack square
or some skirmish or foray

These bemedalled gentlemen in their
tunics of scarlet
tell of many an epic not easy to forget
their colourful decorations paint
a picture of many a campaign
in some strange and far-off terrain
coming from all regiments
of the line
and though elderly, they are still
men of bearing, upright and fine

This unique and unusual society
adding yet more spice to London's variety
this community of gallant men,
much praise and glory have they won
with their share of active service
and duty done
and though the swarming millions
of the metropolis may mingle
and crowd
these veterans stand out stalwart and proud

Village Scene (Blackheath)

Looking across this green expanse
one can see the village church
and steeple
seeming far away in the distance
and not looking part of this vast
City, with its never ending suburbs
and teeming people
but, as one draws nearer and nearer
the tumult and hubbub
of town life drones
and gets clearer and clearer
until reaching quite deafening tones

With all the vehicular traffic of
City life
its individuality it cannot keep
as this noisy mass runs rife
while more and more, through
its high street continues to sweep
but one can escape the clatters
and the dins
on this placid heath a-strolling-to-go
even when the wintry fury begins
to join in the seasonal games
on its smooth carpet of snow

International Air Base

Jets streaking skywards
almost, straight from the ground
jets streaking upwards
with a screeching and thund'ring sound
others sweeping downwards
on the runways to ride
some preparing for the take-off
their engines warming and whistling
and while waiting for the lift off
their crews with activity bristling

Strange and varied are these aircraft
their engines immense and powerful
some forward, some their engines aft
with exhausts discharging forceful
raising these giants without difficulty
trailing their fumes across the sky
surging with velocity
disappearing like a speck, like a fly
to the world's many cities
above many a mountain peak
like huge flying taxis
as here from the tarmac they streak

At this international air base
in the heart of London's countryside
'tis a most exciting and interesting place
adding more to the Capital's pride
industrious as a beehive
this once rustic place has become

yet, 'tis not bees that arrive
though they drone and hum
almost a town of its own
with its offices, restaurants and shops
so much has it overgrown
this, one of the world's busiest air stops

The Hall

Oh! how for the promenade concerts
they queue
to hear the music of the masters
to pass comment on a work
that is new
or to applaud their favourite
conductors

Many others crowd here also
from City, town and village
from all parts of the country
to hear the massed bands play
in championship style and tempo
and cheer their local musicians
in victory

Followed by their fans who demand
excitement plus fair play
come the boxing community
to display the art of
self-defence and skill
choral societies too, have their day
with fervour, singing to their fill

So they queue for the many events
that take place here
and here too, in remembrance
the poppies fall
in the latter part of the year
across the way from Kensington Park
under the great dome of the Albert Hall

Scrubbs Carnival

Roll up, roll up, all the fun of the fair
all the sound of merriment
floating across the holiday air
buses packed with children
who, down the stairs come tumbling
their faces lit with excitement
do not hear the conductor's grumbling
eager to see the sideshows
or try the swings and roundabouts
and the gay tumult grows and grows
almost drowning the laughter and shouts
all kinds of mechanical fun providing
hung roundabout with fairylighting
dodgem cars colliding
Oh 'tis so delighting
shots, from the rifle range ringing
maybe 'tis toy balloons that sound
jovial crowds singing
Oh the gaiety at this scrubland fairground

Cricket Pitch

Have you ever been to Lord's, this
stately home of English cricket
and what exciting moment do you recall
and what great batsman at the wicket
trying to prevent its fall
maybe just a league game
or perhaps a vital test match
being staged
with some gentlemen of fame
from the West Indies, Pakistan
or Australia, being engaged

Lord's, cricket's metropole elite, and
home of the coveted ashes trophy
with its pitch trimmed a close crop
smooth green and velvety
looking, more like a billiard table top
here, many have scored their
"hundred not out"
in a skilled batting display
and a haven too, where the town birds
love to flit about
at the end of play

The Men in Blue

Many a story is told, of these fine
men, brave and bold
smartly dressed in blue
with an upright bearing too
stalwart and steady, always alert
always at the ready
and if one's in trouble, the people's friend
a helping hand he will always lend

No matter whatever his function
on duty at some busy junction
and too, when sporting crowds go astray
he is there to see fair play
when demonstrators come to wrangle
he has to sort out the tangle
but the men who make up the Force
take it all as a matter of course

Coming, as they do, from village
town, and other Cities too
a star attraction is he
to the visitor from overseas
some may inquire from him "the time"
while he is there to combat crime
with his exploits first rate, not secondary
why! he is almost legendary

Ancient and Modern

How nice, in this day and age
when rockets, and space ships
are all the rage
to see, almost any day
a horse-drawn brewery dray
laden with a cargo of good cheer
of wine casks, of barrels of beer
clip-clopping through the busy
thoroughfares
causing a stir of interest
causing a few stares
leading an assortment of motor vehicles
in slow procession
as they make steady progression
around to the many taverns and inns
to replenish stocks
before drinking time begins

The Volcano

Once one of the Celtic settlements
until over-run by the Roman regiments
who built their City, as one recalls
but which has long overflowed
its protective walls

This metropolis, still spreading so
like the lava of a great volcano
its centre bubbling with activity
but slackening to the suburbs
gradually

With eight million population or so
and still continuing to grow
as the great brick and mortar tide
overspills into the surrounding
countryside

Seemingly its energy cannot be spent
forcing into Middlesex, Surrey, Essex and Kent
and, as if having no remorse
engulfing farms, villages and towns as it
goes its multiple course

Where will it stop? One has their fears
continuing its expansion over the years
but where will it stop eventually?
It may, one dreads to think, finally
reach down to the sea

Lofty Dwelling

Ah, if I but had the power
I would purchase the post office tower
what a lofty dwelling I would
have taken
what a wonderful place in which
to awaken
what a panorama on which to gaze
though perhaps not always with
London's smoggy haze

From my unique and exciting home
I would see St Paul's and its great dome
and the Thames, glinting in the distance
like a jewel
with the Tower Bridge crossing
its busy pool
and still in the east
looking very American
the skyscraper development of Barbican

Gazing out with fascination
at this fine view of St Pancras station
with trains coming and going
at all hours of the day
looking more like a model railway
I would see the ornate frontage of
King's Cross terminus as well
which, so I am told was once
a thriving hotel

Looking further northwards still
one would see the village of
Highgate upon the hill
charming and old fashioned yet
something, which some of us
do not regret
and in the misty distance beyond
that television station known affectionately
to many as Ally Pally

The North West looking rather green
much open space and grassland
can be seen
elegant Regent's Park with its zoo
its lake and Queen Mary's Gardens too
overlooking, though not forgetting
Primrose Hill, I'd see Parliament Hill
its fields adjoining Hampstead Heath
its lush greeness unspoilt still

Turning my gaze to the West
and wondering where my eyes
would come to rest
maybe on St James', Spanish Place
that beautiful place of worship
any town or City would it grace
or maybe Broadcasting House
as they are reading the News
interesting perhaps, but not one of the
finer views

Across the way from the Hyde Park greenery
I might have to strain to see
the circular contour of
the Albert Hall
perhaps here, happy memories
for some to recall

and looking from here like
a desert fort
that concrete monster at Earls Court

Looking South, looking into history
filled with wonderment and mystery
there, visible, the Mother of Parliaments
and House of national pride
and too the old County Hall on
the opposite river side
not forgetting, the smiling faces
of Big Ben
with Nelson's column looking
more like a biro pen

Still in the same vicinity, Westminster
Abbey, that ancient monument
of Christianity
visible too, though some distance apart
The Cathedral, its more modern counterpart
and on the far bank as the river bends
looking like a giant birthday cake,
but not as pleasant to see
the Power House sending out
its dynamic energy

Looking down at the traffic flow
at the red omnibus monsters
looking mere playtoys below
and people hurrying, full of zest
as though, ants from a pavement nest
Ah! if such property were mine
a big smile I would beam
but I'm afraid, that could only be
a pleasant dream

Crosstalk

Early each morning, barrow-boy Fred
rolls out of his "uncle ned"
and having no worries or cares
makes his way down the apples and pears
a busy man is he, who soon empties
a quick cup of rosie lee
and still with a jaunty air
sets to combing his barnet fair
with the completion of that
puts on his tit for tat
and while everyone else upstairs
continues to snore
quietly slips out through
the Rory O'Moore

Though it may be cold
and chilling to the marrow
he grabs hold of his bow and arrow
and with his fruity load
sets off down the frog and toad
all day long at his pitch he stands
with fruit or veg in his german bands
and in the evening
at the local, his pals he will greet
after a hard day on his plates of meat
and too, with the light of his life
his dear lady, his struggle and strife
and wishing all around good cheer
quickly downs a pint of frothy pig's ear

At week-ends he looks cute
dressed in his best whistle and flute
though not to be a dandy, does he crave
when also he has a close dig in the grave
and, as he is not in the red
because, he uses his loaf of bread
takes his missus, smartly dressed too,
to dine, where there is a tasty
me and you
not minding the expense incurred
he doesn't grumble, he doesn't say
a dicky bird
always to remember his better half
is his plan
and he is to her, her dear old pot and pan

Waxen Wonder

Oh! how lifelike do these models appear
and though they are not real
yet I fear, much of the limelight
do they steal
for day after day
whether in sunshine or snow
come visitors from over the seas
from countries far away
to see the world's greatest waxwork show

There they stand, the famous
and the infamous
all receiving equal praise
yet quite unaware of the fuss
and the public's admiring gaze
they are but waxen, made
by experts to this unusual trade
and where else or when
have you seen such craft displayed

Each having a pitch of their own
Statesmen, sportsmen, inventors, lawbreakers
all are here!
the finest collection known
covering almost every career
soldiers, airmen, navigators too
some perhaps, great pioneers
stand here on review, but cannot now
acknowledge acclaiming cheers

Some sought to build an empire
were once high and mighty
who tried the world to acquire
now stand as a mere effigy
however, if on a visit one day
the attendant does not reply to you
when you have inquired your way
do not be surprised, for he may be
just a model too!

Birdsong

Many are the birds I have heard
in Berkeley Square
though, there was no nightingale
the last time that I was there
but others were chirping and singing
from the rooftops
of the high buildings around
or flitting, from the twigs
of the branches of the tall trees
overhanging the lawn below
and the continuous shiny stream
of taxis darting to and fro

"Twickers"

Have you ever watched s scrum
at "Twickers"
where the flame of England's rugby,
flickers
have you ever joined the
enthusiastic files
swarming through the clicking
turnstiles
to support Oxford and Cambridge
Universities
in a tough and thrilling 'varsity'
or go there as well
to see an exciting and stirring
international
with a virile team from the
Emerald Isle
or a French captain leading his
team out, with a confident smile
maybe a team of hardy Scots
or the singing Welshmen,
who hope to tie the home team
up in knots

The Londoner

The native of London City
is a cosmopolitan personality
his grandparents may have come
from The Emerald Isle,
he will tell you with a smile
another bystander will be the son
of a fiery Highlander
or another, the son of a miner
from the land of green hills
and golden daffodils
yet another will tell you, that
he is English through and through

The proprietor of some High Street jewellers
may be descended from
a refugee Jew
the London born family of Andreas
in his fish bar, will be citizens
of the Metropolis too
Luigi or Pierre restaurateurs
their sons and daughters will become
Londoners as well
and there are many more people
of whom I could write and tell
for, this most prosperous of cities
has attracted many nationalities

Tyburn Walk

People stop in surprise
why this silent and orderly
procession?
they can hardly believe their eyes
so reverent and without transgression
as it moves through the somewhat
quietened thoroughfares
these men and women, their faith
they profess
without proud or pretentious airs
the most treasured thing they
possess

Moving away from the Old Bailey
on the last Sunday of the fourth
month of the year
as the clock strikes three
about that time, or somewhere near
away down Snow Hill
at quite a leisurely pace
with the men in blue, holding
the impatient motorist still
who sits there revving as though
taking part in a motor race

At Ely Place they pause
when others too join this "stroll"
to honour those who died
for a noble cause
yet would not have their names

put to any honours scroll,
and so to Soho Square
perhaps through an April shower
to sing a hymn and say a prayer
of greater value, than anything
from temporal power

The marchers, with a crucifix held
high, priests, religious and laity
move off again without a shout or cry
'tis no sombre march, nor one of gaiety
ending at Marble Arch
where, all but a stone's throw away
there is for all to see, a tablet by
the roadway, telling of where stood
the infamous 'Tyburn tree'
at this once countryway
now a world famed highway
busy as can be

On this tree, the innocent and the
guilty, had with their lives to pay
the innocent, their enemies they forgave
are remembered here this day
themselves, they did not try to save
for to them 'twas no sorrow
as they praised their Creator
thinking of their glorious tomorrow
and the crowds at the convent near,
too, honour their Maker
disperse, and fade away, to form up
again another year

Busy Thoroughfare (Hammersmith)

Whizzy, busy Broadway
with an assortment of vehicles
seemingly ever flowing
almost any hour of the day
and its density continuously
growing
with no walking space
to be found
motors swamping all and every place
forcing pedestrians underground
with the many toned horns hooting
('tis very much of a rat race I feel)
in all directions shooting
like sparks from a grinding wheel

Babbling Brook

Lowly little Wandle
gently flowing through the streets
of South London
sometimes a mere trickle
with not much of a run
other times, when the rain is falling
how it surges, how it bubbles
as if from some sudden calling
past the traffic at its peak
past the crowds, some gay,
some weary and bowed down
with troubles
yet sweetly as it races
seeming playing hide and seek
showing up at the most odd
and unusual places

Sporting London

At the drop of the national flag
snarling motors spurt forward
and the once tense men at the wheel
now more relaxed but cannot lag
if they are to be the victors
and gain the coveted award
forcing their engines to near
exploding point, and not daring
to look back
forcing them on and on
lap after lap here, at the
Crystal Palace road track
this, one of the many events of sporting
London

In almost any district on a Saturday
you can hear an echoing roar
carried by the wind
over the rooftops, through the streets
and away
'tis the sound of the many
enthusiastic soccer fans
urging their team on
to perhaps yet another score
and though it may be wintry
with sleet and flakes of snow
with temperatures like that of a 'fridge'
the keenness of the crowds does not slow
be it at White Hart Lane
or Stamford Bridge

Up the trap doors fly
away tear the eager hounds
to catch the deceptive hare, they try
away, away with no bounds
past the crowds agog with eagerness
past those chappies "in the know"
for they have the winner
and do not guess
yet have nothing to show
and the chase goes on with intent
until that elusive piece of fur
disappears from the floodlight glow
with both the energy of the dogs
and money of the punters being spent
at the stadium at Walthamstow

Like the ticking of some clock
the ball whizzes over the net
back and forth, tick tock, tick tock
from racquet to racquet
maybe a title is at stake
with some newcomer
to spring a surprise
seemingly as there by mistake
but a budding champion in disguise
still, whatever the outcome
at the centre court
as from many lands they come and go
one may wonder if instead of sport
it looks more like a fashion show

Six to four the field,
the bookies cry
and the undecided punter wonders
should he to the temptation yield
or let the next race go by
still he might win,

should there be a hitch
but 'tis only the bookies that grin
'tis only they that get rich
still 'tis interesting to watch everyone
trying to make their mark
and the antics of the tipsters
with their chatter and their moves
amidst the excitement of thundering
hooves, at Kempton Park

Like a clap of thunder
away from the starting tapes they roar
clad in helmets and leathery armour
each determined to get to the fore
into the bend they sweep
astride their revving and
powerful mounts
jockeying for position
and keep in the place that counts
Oh the excitement is never failing
and the foursome, ending four exerting
laps, cinders spraying
whether foot forward or leg trailing
streak for the victor's place
in this the final run
amidst the urging and claps
this, another event of sporting London

The Village Pond

There's one place I'll not be forgetting
'tis almost country-like in its setting
for how nice it is at Barnes
to sit by the village pond
to watch or feed the ducks and swans
with the trees and bushes
of the common beyond
'tis so calm and serene
this still and rustic scene
away from the chaos and rush
a fitting subject for some artist's
eager brush

Rustic City

It is not as it would seem
miles and miles of concrete
as if some unpleasant dream
for many are the parks
and little patches of green
where no building is or has ever been
where the glory of spring overspills
with crocus, tulips and daffodils
No, it is not as one supposes
as one watches the never tiring bees
amongst the summery roses
or the many tinted leaves in flight
doing an autumnal dance
around a lamp standard
or traffic light

Rabbits and squirrels
not counting those at the zoo
find their homes on the heaths
and open spaces too
and then again you would hardly
call this rare,
pigeons in Trafalgar Square
and in the Broadway at Hammersmith
starlings making merry
seagulls circling Woolwich ferry
seems as if one was speaking
about some farm
this City of rustic charm